Wow

Words photos & illustrations

by Junko

Contents 目次

Preface　はじめに	6
Chapter 1:　Awakening ～目覚め～	8
Chapter 2:　Observation ～観察～	60
Chapter 3:　Acceptance ～現状把握～	112
Chapter 4:　Moving Forward ～前進～	164
Coda　おわりに	216
About The Author　著者について	217

Preface

I have loved writing and drawing since I was a child. But I forgot about this joy once I became an adult when a busy life took over. Around 2012, I went through a series of painful experiences, that now I can call "opportunities" to lose lots of things that were no longer serving me. Since then, I slowly regained only the meaningful things in my life and I have started spending time doing what I've always loved. Now I'm full of words and ideas. I write naturally and draw like a kid.

My wish is for many people in the world to read my book. That's why I wrote in English first. English is not my first language but I used easy words that people like me can understand and study from this book. And the reason I wrote in Japanese was by using my own language, I could express myself to the fullest.

This book is about what I've learned not only from those difficult times, but also from my 50 years of life so far. My learning and discovery will never stop until I finish this life on earth. Please don't read this book too quickly. Read one page at a time, skip pages, keep going back to certain pages or just forget about words and enjoy the pictures.

Hopefully this book can make you feel at ease, go for your dreams, reduce your stress, start to love yourself, or admit that you're doing okay so that you can enjoy your life's journey. I believe our collective peace of mind creates world peace. Let's start from each of us.

Arigato,
   Junko

はじめに

思えば私は小さな頃から、文字を書いたり絵を描くのが好きでした。でも大人になり、日々の多忙さからそんな楽しさをすっかり忘れて過ごしていました。しかし、2012年頃に大切だと思っていたたくさんのものを失うという不運（今思えば、もう必要なくなったものを失くすことができたという幸運）が重なり、その頃からもともと自分が好きだったことを少しずつ始めてみました。今では私の頭の中には言葉やアイデアが溢れているので、文章を気軽に書いたり子供のように絵を描いて楽しんでいます。

私は世界中のなるべく多くの人々にこの本を読んで頂きたく思い、まずは簡単な英語を使って書いてみました。英語を母国語としない私のような人達にも、この本から英語を学んで頂ければと思います。更に、自らの母国語である日本語を併用することによって、私は本当の自分を自由に表現できたと思っています。

この本にある言葉は最近の事柄からだけではなく、私のこれまでの人生50年全ての経験から学んだレッスンです。私の学びと発見はこれからもこの世を去る時まで続きます。この本は急いで読まないで下さい。1ページずつゆっくり見たり、またはページを飛ばしたり、お気に入りのところだけ何度も読んだり、あるいは文字を気にせず写真だけでもお楽しみ下さい。

私の本が、少しでも多くの人々を楽にでき、夢に向かう人達を応援し、日常のストレスを減らし、皆様が自分を大切にして自信を持って楽しく生きられるようお手伝いできたら嬉しいです。私は世界平和は私達個人の心の平和から作り出せれるものだと信じています。それぞれができることから始めていきましょう。

感謝をこめて、
Junko

Feel your heartbeat

You're alive now,
 alive at this moment.
Place your hand on your heart
 and recognize your heartbeat.
You certainly exist here now.

あなたの鼓動を確認しよう

あなたは今日生きている
今ここに生きている
心臓に手を当てて
自分の鼓動を確認しよう
あなたは今 確かに存在する

Appreciate your life everyday

Unfortunately,
some of us didn't make it until today.
But you did.
You made it.
You're alive!
Isn't that fact already wonderful?

毎日命があることに感謝しよう．

残念ながら
今日まで生きてこれなかった人達もいる．
なのにあなたは生きている．
それだけでまず奇跡．
それだけでとても素晴らしいこと．

Enjoy every color in your life

What do you notice when you look around?
White walls,
blue sky,
yellow sunflowers...
Focus on every color you see
and enjoy the difference.

人生の全ての色彩を楽しもう

見回したら何が見える？
白い壁、
青い空、
黄色いひまわり、
あらゆる色に注目して
その違いを楽しもう。

Do what you love

You feel that time flies
 when you're doing what you love.
Enjoy yourself
 without thinking about time
and become more skillful as you continue.
 ♪ Start spending time
  doing what you really like
  and get lost in it.

好きなことをしよう

自分の好きなことをしていると
知らないうちに時が流れてゆき.
楽しんで時間を過ごすことができる.
だからこそ 続けられる. ♪
続けられると上達する.
まずは 好きなことをして過ごし
我を忘れてみよう. ♪

Laugh everyday

Laughing is a wonderful thing.
Happiness comes to those who laugh often.
Others receive your happy vibes
through your laughter.
And you will attract marvelous things
to your life from laughter.

毎日笑おう

笑うこと。
笑うことって素晴らしい
笑う門には本当に福が来る。
楽しい思いは空気で伝わる。
素敵な物事が
あなたの笑いで引き寄せられて来る。

Walking is great for your soul.

Sceneries slowly change as you walk.
you move forward
both mentally and physically.
Open your eyes and
discover countless things
when you're just walking.

歩くことは精神的にも効果あり。

歩いてゆくと
目に映るものが少しずつ変わりながら
あなたの心も体も前へ進んで行く。
歩いているだけで
たくさんの発見がある

Pause and enjoy
the sight, smell and sound of your surroundings.

Spend a precious moment
noticing flowers on the street...
Stop and smell them
Enjoy everything that surrounds you
with all your five senses.
Don't miss anything beautiful
by going too fast.

立ち止まり、身の回りの景色、匂い、音を楽しもう

外を歩いて道端のお花を見つけ
立ち止まり、その香りを楽しむような
贅沢な時間を過ごそう。
身の回りのあらゆるものを
五感で感じよう。
急ぎすぎて素敵な物事を
見落とさないように

どこにいても自分なりの平和を見つけよう

大自然の中にいるならもちろんのこと。
人混みの中にも
オフィスにも
平和は存在する。
美味しい紅茶を飲んだ朝。
それは平和。

座り心地のいい椅子に座っている自分。
それもまた平和。
小さな平和は私達の身の回りに
たくさん存在する。

Solitude is a rich experience.

Don't feel lonely when you're alone.
There are many things that you can do
only when you're alone.
There are people who would be
      envious of your solitude.
It's the best time for you
        to be creative.
Use your time sagely.

孤独とは贅沢な時間.

一人でいることは寂しいことではない.
一人でいる時にしかできないことはたくさんある.
世の中には、あなたが一人でいるその時間を
羨ましいと思う人達が大勢いる.
一人の時間は、何かを創り出すには最高の時間.
上手く活用しよう.

Taste the air.
Listen to the wind.

Think about the things you don't see
that you could be taking for granted.
Air tastes differently
 depending on the place or season.
A soft breeze can only move grass
 but a gale can be heard even when
  you're indoors.
Appreciate all the things
 you don't normally observe.

They're here just like we exist on earth.

空気を味わい、風の音を聞こう

目に見えないもの、普段注目さえしていなかったもの、
そういうものたちの存在を改めて考えてみよう。
場所や季節によって空気の味は違う。
そよ風は草を揺らし、強い風は家の中にいても聞こえる。
目に見えなくても存在している無数のものたちに改めて感謝。
地球自体が私達と共に生きている。

Express your gratitude.

If someone is nice to you,
 thank them.
It's never too late to say thank you
 no matter how long it's been.
Be grateful when good things happen to you.
 You can express your gratitude
  by words or attitude.
 Think about all the things
  that you feel thankful for.

感謝の気持ちを示そう.

誰かに何かをしてもらったら
必ずお礼を言おう
それがどんなに前のことでも
遅すぎることはない.
何か嬉しいことがあったら
感謝の気持ちを示し
それは言葉だけでなく
態度にも自分の生き方にも示すことができる.
自分は何に対してありがたいと思っているか
意識してみよう

Be pure, be frugal

Don't forget to be humble,
pure and simple.
Things aren't usually as complicated
as they seem.
So be simple-minded
to deal with them.

純粋で素朴にいこう

いつも純粋な気持ちを忘れず
質素に素朴にいこう。
物事は一見複雑に見えても
実際は単純かもしれない、
だからシンプルに対応しよう

Use what you have.

Instead of focusing on
what you don't have,
think about what you have,
and what you can do with it.
Start using everything
that's already there
and see how it goes.

持っているものを使おう.

あれがない
これがない
ではなくて、
まずここに何があるのか！
このままのあなたに何ができるのかを考え.
既に持っているものから
大いに活用しよう.

Start with one.

When you have so many things that
you want to do or you don't know what to do,
Start with one thing that is right in front of you.
Start with something you're good at.
Start with anything easy.
That will keep you going forward.
That will give you strength.

何か一つから始めよう

やりたいことや
やるべきことがたくさんありすぎる時
または何をしていいか全然わからない時
自分の目の前にあること、
得意なこと、
または簡単に始められることから
一つだけやってみよう。
一つずつやってみよう。
その継続は力となる。

Believe

Believe in yourself.
Believe in your ability.
Believe in your passion.
Believe in your power and possibilities.
Believe in what you enjoy and what you imagine.
Believe in your hopes, dreams and happy self.
If you can believe in one thing,
things will start to change.
As long as you believe,
anything is possible!

信じよう.

自分を信じよう.
自分の能力を信じよう.
自分の情熱を信じよう.
自分の力、
可能性、
楽しめること、
想像すること、
夢、
希望、
幸せな自分の姿を信じよう.
一つでも信じられたら、
物事は変わり始める.
信じる限り全ては可能。

Love yourself
before you love others.

If you don't love yourself,
no one will understand how great you are.
Find one thing you like about yourself
and start loving the fact.
Realize the true value of your being
and how exquisite you are
to love yourself more than ever.

他人を愛する前に
自分を愛そう

自分をダメな人間だと思っていたら
あなたの魅力は誰にも伝わらない。
まず一つでも自分の良いところを見つけ
自分のことを好きになろう。
この世にたった一人しかいない自分の価値に気づけたら
あなたはもっと自分を好きになれる。

Curiosity makes you smarter.

When you find yourself being curious about something new, follow your interest. Knowledge is limitless. You'll never know when you'll have opportunities to use what you learn. Your possibilities will be widened.

興味や関心は
あなたを更に賢くする.

何か新しいことに心惹かれたら
それを追求してみよう
知識はどれだけあっても
ありすぎるということはない.
いつ何に活用できるかわからない.
豊富な知識はあなたの可能性を
更に広げる.

Give yourself a reward.

Be gentle to yourself
for making an effort everyday.
Take care of your stress and pain.
Give yourself a reward
  and praise for doing a great job.

自分にご褒美をあげよう

日々頑張りすぎている自分を労ってあげよう。
日々疲れている自分をゆっくり休めてあげよう。
自分にちょっとしたご褒美をあげて励ましてあげよう、
いつもありがとう、そしてお疲れ様、と
自分に声をかけてあげよう。

Dream big
The world is all yours

Dreams have no limit.
You can dream anything
on a worldwide scale.
No one has a right to judge your dreams.
Your dreams have so many possibilities.
Don't limit yourself.
Be free to dream big.

世界規模の大きな夢を持とう

夢の大きさに制限はない。
世界規模の夢を持ったっていい。
他人には笑う権利もない。
あなたの夢は無限の可能性を秘めている。
限りなく自由に夢を見よう。

Look forward to something good happening.

You'll be in a great mood
if you're looking forward to something.
People will sense positive frequencies
in your excitement,
and wonderful things will
come your way.

何か良いことが起こると
楽しみにしていよう．

楽しみなことが目先にあると
何事にも頑張ることができる．
そして そのわくわくドキドキは
周りにも伝わって
あなたに必ず素敵なことが起こる．

You don't have to meet anyone's expectations. Just follow your heart.

Don't try to please everyone.
You'll lose your true self
if you try to meet others' expectations.
Think first before you act.
Is it for you or someone else?
Ask yourself
and follow your heart.

誰の期待にも沿わず、自分の心に従おう。

誰かを喜ばそうとしなくていい。
皆の期待に応えることだけを考えて進むと
本当の自分とは全く別人になってしまう。
誰のために行動しているのか
自分は何をしたいのか
よく考えていこう。

Your imperfections make you who you are.

Perfect or imperfect are the words used
when we compare ourselves with others.
We're different and no one's perfect.
Our differences make everything interesting
and make the world more fun.
The imperfections are our personality.

あなたの不完全さこそが
あなたの個性。

私達は他と何かを比べた時だけ
完全か不完全かという表現を使う。
でも実際、私達は完全、不完全ではなく
皆それぞれが他人と違うだけ。
完璧な人間なんてどこにもいない。
皆違うからこそ全ては興味深くなり、
世界は楽しいものになる。
不完全さは私達の個性。

Trust your own decisions.

When you come to a decision,
respect it and trust your own mind.
If you take time to know
what you'd like to do,
just go for it without a doubt.

自分の決断を信じよう.

何か決めたら
自分がたどり着いたその決断を信じていこう.
ゆっくり時間をかけて決心したのなら
迷うことはない.

Let yourself go with the wind

Imagine yourself floating with the winds or waves.
Be weightless and let them take you away.
If you fight against the stream,
you won't go anywhere,
but if you go with the flow,
you'll reach the place where you're supposed to be.

風に吹かれるままにいこう。

風に吹かれるように
波に流されるように
自然の流れに身を委ねてみよう。
流れに抵抗しても疲れるだけで前へは進めない。
でも流れは優しくあなたの背中を押す。
物事の流れに沿えば、
あなたは行くべきところへ到達する。

Walk, don't run

Be steadfast,
Walk slow.
Step by step,
walk on.
Don't miss anything
by going too fast.

走らずに歩こう

一歩一歩着実に地に足をつけて
自分のペースで歩いて行こう。
急ぎすぎて大切なものを
見逃さないように。

Chapter 2: Observation
～観察～

Focus on your happy thoughts.

What makes you happy?
Focus on your pleasant thoughts.
You'll spend your time smiling.

楽しい思いに焦点を当てよう

どんなことを考えたら幸せな気持ちになれるだろう.
楽しい思考に焦点を当てると
わくわくして笑顔で時間を過ごすことができる

Observe yourself nonjudgmentally.

There is no good or bad.
There is no right or wrong.
Observe yourself calmly
and accept yourself
nonjudgmentally
Just be gentle to who you are.

自分自身を非難することなく観察してみよう。

良い悪い。
正しい正しくない。
そんな判断なしに
単に自分とはどのような人間なのか
ゆっくり観察してみよう。
そしてそのままの自分を優しく受け入れよう。

Be simple.
Don't complicate things.

Things just happen,
but we add our own
　　　opinions and feelings
to make them complicated.
Instead of wrapping them
　　　with worries and fears,
just go back to the fact that
things just happen、

物事を複雑にせず
　　　シンプルにいこう、

人生に起こる様々なことは
実は単純なことばかりかもしれないのに、
そこに自分の思考が加わると
すぐに複雑で難しいものに変っていく、
心配や不安で簡単なことを困難にしないよう
基本に帰ってみよう、

Stay here now
with your body and mind.

Enjoy the beautiful scenery
when you're in nature.
Don't ruin the richness
by thinking about
what you have to do tomorrow.
Focus on using all your senses
to enjoy everything fully.

心も体もこの場所にいよう

せっかく綺麗な大自然の中にいても
明日の仕事のことばかり考えていたのでは勿体ない
安らげる場所では特に色彩や香りに集中して
全身全霊で楽しもう.

Embrace the moment. Everything is art.

Live in the moment and admire the colors when you find an autumn foliage on the street. We're surrounded by a lot of gorgeous things. Let's notice them as we live on.

その時その時を大切にしよう、全てはアートである.

ふと道端の落ち葉を見た時
その形や色合いに感動できるよう
一瞬一瞬を大切に生きよう.
私達は沢山の美しいものに囲まれて生きている.
その素晴らしさに気付きながらいこう.

Don't lie to yourself

Sometimes you may find yourself
doing something against your will.
Therefore, always listen to your heart.
You'll be going in the right direction.

自分に嘘をつかないようにしよう。

気がついたら自分の心とは裏腹なことをしていた経験は
誰にでもあるかもしれない。
だから常に心の声を聞き
自分に問いかけながらいこう。
本当の自分の姿で進めば
行くべきところへたどり着く。

Look around and see what inspires you.

Look around carefully
and see what excites and influences you,
what motivates and inspires you.
Just look around mindfully.

周りを見渡して、
自分に良い影響を与えている物を知ろう。

あなたの置かれた環境をゆっくり見渡して
一体自分は何に興味がそそられ
どんなことに影響（インスパイア）されるのか
自分と周囲の両方を観察してみよう。

Choose your friends wisely.

Your life depends on what kind of people you spend time with.
Surround yourself with people
who bring you joy,
who support you,
with whom you can share your joy.
If you're with those who have a rich imagination
with hopes and dreams,
they'll influence you divinely.

友達選びは慎重にしよう.

どんな人達に関わっていくか
どんな人達が周りにいるかで
私達の人生は大きく変わってゆく。
あなたの幸せを喜んでくれる人達、
あなたの決断を応援してくれる人達、
夢や希望に溢れる想像豊かな人達が周りにいたら
あなたの生活は素敵に影響されてゆく。

Exchange opinions instead of arguing.

It's natural that everyone has a different opinion.
Respect others and learn from them.
Nothing starts from arguments,
but by exchanging your opinions,
you can add new ideas to your thinking.
That may lead you to an unexpected good result.

言い争うのではなく、意見を交換しよう

人それぞれ意見は違って当たり前。
人々の意見を尊重して そこから学んでいこう。
口論しても 何も始まらないが
意見を交換することにより
相手の良い部分を自分に取り入れることもできる。
自分では考えもしなかったようなことを耳にしても
それが思わぬ良い結果に繋がるかもしれない。

A simple "Hello" can lead you to lots of great things

Always remember to greet people.
Think about how wonderful exchanging greetings is.
A simple "Hello" can lead you to a deeper conversation.
You could be invited to an incredible place,
or may end up being able to get a great job.
You'll always gain something
when you have good manners.

簡単な挨拶は数々の良いことに繋がっていく。

挨拶は忘れずにしよう。
声をかけること、かけ合うことの素晴らしさを考えてみよう。
単に「こんにちは」から話が弾み、
あなたは素敵な場所へ招かれるかもしれない。
良い仕事に就けるかもしれない。
マナーあるところに実りあり。

Free yourself from your own rules.

Without realizing,
we're all making our own rules
based on our common sense and experiences.
We're limiting our possibilities
and making ourselves suffer by doing so.
Consequently, if you recognize your pattern,
rethink about how you are going to be.
Soften your restrictions
and set yourself free.

自分ルールから解放されよう

長い経験に基づいて
私達は気付かぬうちに自分勝手に色々なルールを作っている。
知らないうちに物事を決めつけて
自分を苦しめていることに気付いたら
自分を改めてみよう。
決まり事をなるべく減らして
自らをストレスから解放しよう。

Doing nothing is also an option.

You don't always have to do something.
Doing nothing is one of your choices.
It's okay to leave it be.

何もしないという選択もある.

いつも何かをしないといけないというわけではない.
何もしないことを選ぶのも行動のうち、
そんな選択もあって良い.

Surround yourself with people who believe in you.

If you're surrounded with people
who trust your words
and believe in your dreams
and possibilities,
you'll reach your goal sooner.

あなたを信じてくれる人達の中に
自分を位置付けよう

あなたの言葉を信じてくれる人達.
あなたの可能性や夢を疑わない人達に
囲まれると

やりたいことに一層早く近付ける.

Make the person in the mirror happy
before you try to help others.

If you find yourself doing something for others,
or you can't find time for yourself,
you can stop whatever you're doing.

If you can't find a happy self in the mirror,
the first thing you need to do is
to take care of yourself

人助けをする前に
まず鏡の中の自分を幸せにしよう

気づいたら誰かのために何かをしていて
自分の事がいつも後回しになっている等
他人中心に動いている自分を見つけたら
まずは止まろう
毎朝鏡を覗き込んだ時
そこに幸せな自分が見えなければ
あなたのやるべきことは
まず自分を幸せにすること

Be with people who can expand your world.

It would be a wonderful relationship if they're expanding your world, but it would be inappropriate if you're limited. Check on your relationship with people with whom you surround yourself and how they're influencing you.

あなたの世界観が広がるような人達と一緒にいよう

その人といて自分の視野も行動範囲も広がるようなら
それは素晴らしい人間関係と言えよう。
その人といて自分のやりたいことが限定されるようなら
それは望ましい関係ではないかもしれない。
自分の世界が広がっているか制限されているか
人との繋がりをそれぞれ確認してみよう。

Mind and body are two different things. Listen to both.

Even if you think you're okay in your mind,
you might be physically saying "No".
Don't miss any small signs that your body is giving you.
Take good care of both your mind and body.

心と体は別々のもの 両方の声を聞いていこう

頭では大丈夫と思っていても
体が悲鳴を上げていることもある
だから小さなサインも逃さず
両方のバランスを見ながら
物事を進めてゆくのが大事

You are in a **Mess** ???

Message

You're okay!

Junko

Zoom out to see the whole picture.

You can't see the whole picture if you're too close to the subject.
Try to see your situation with an objective point of view.
Pretend that you're up in the air and look down on yourself.
You'll be able to see many things around you that you couldn't see before.

There might be a support system or friends who are willing to help you,
there might be a detour or other ways to solve the problem.
Even if you think you're at a deadend, there is always a way for you.

遠く離れて全体を客観視してみよう

近付きすぎると全体像が見えない.
だから敢えて物事から距離を置いて
自分の位置も含めて確認してみよう.
あなたの現在の状況をもし空の上から見たとしたら
普段見えなかった色々な援助や応援してくれる人達が
周りに見えてくるかもしれない.

問題の真っ只中へ直進しなくても
他の道や回り道が見えてくるかもしれない.
どんな状況も決して行き止まりではない.

Give yourself permission to rest. You deserve it.

It's okay to give yourself permission to rest
because you've been working very hard.
No one else would do that if you don't do it for yourself.
It's okay to rest.
You deserve it.
Take good care of yourself.

自分を休ませてあげよう
あなたにはその価値がある

こんなに頑張って来たのだから
今日はゆっくり休んでいいよ、と自分に言ってあげよう。

あなたが自分自身に許可しない限り
誰もそんなことを言ってくれないかもしれない。

あなたは休んでもいい。
あなたにはその価値がある。
自分を大切にしよう。

Stop overthinking and live in the "now"

Thinking has no limits.
We have more than 60,000 thoughts a day.
That's why there is no point in overthinking.
You can't do anything about
your past or future at this moment.
If you find yourself thinking too much,
shift your attention to the present.
Just embrace what your eyes can see
and enjoy being in the moment.

考えすぎず今を楽しもう

考え続けてもキリがない。
人は一日に6万から8万ものことを考えている。
だからこそ考えすぎても意味はない。
先のことも後のことも今この時点ではどうにもできない
だから考えすぎている自分に気付いたら、
その心の行方を今現在に戻して
目の前のもの、今この時を楽しもう。

Don't let your hesitation block your possibilities

Hesitation, shyness or lack of confidence can limit your own possibilities.
Tell yourself that you're doing okay.
If you think you can't, you won't be able to,
but if you think you can, you'll be able to do it.
Your thoughts create reality.
Control them with caution.

ためらいで あなたの可能性を 妨げないようにしよう

ためらい、恥じらい、自信の無さから
せっかくの可能性を制限してしまうことがある
だから自分に大丈夫だよと言ってあげよう
ダメだと思えばダメになり
できると思えばできる
思考は全てを作り出す
自分から上手くコントロールしよう

Pay attention to what you secretly wish for.

We all have secret wishes.
You think people would laugh at you
or they'd think you're crazy if you tell them.
Our hopes and dreams could be easily ruined
by careless words from others.
That's why keep your secret wishes secret.
Focus on them and know yourself.

自分がこっそり望んでいることに注目してみよう.

人に話すと笑われる、叶うわけないと馬鹿にされる、
そんな他人には言えない秘密の願い事が
私達の心の奥底に潜んでいる.
他人が発する軽い言葉によって
あなたの夢や希望は台無しにも成り得る、
だから誰にも言わずにこっそりと
心の中で自分の信じる理想を作っていこう.
本当の自分が望むものは何なのか
よく考えてみよう

Be kind to every living thing.

Animals, insects, flowers and trees are
all alive just like we are.
Nothing lasts forever
and we live our life with all our heart.
Be gentle to every living thing
even when no one's watching.
We're all pals living at the same time
on this planet earth.

生きるもの全てに優しくしよう

動物も虫も花も木も私達と同じように生きている
永遠なものは何もなく
皆それぞれが与えられた限りある命を一生懸命生きている。
だから誰も見ていなくても
この世に生きる全てのものに優しく接していこう。
皆、今という貴重な時間を
この地球上で一緒に生きる仲間なのだから

Find new friends at any age

Friends won't always be your friends
no matter how long you've known them.
People change and even you change
as life moves forward.
That's why it's important
to find new friends at any age
to expand your world.

いくつになっても新しい友達を見つけよう.

どんなに長い間友達だった人でも
一生友達でいられるとは限らない
人は変わり、自分も変わってゆく.
だからこそ 何歳になっても
新しい友達を作って
自らの世界を広げていこう.

「Your life is made of all your choices.」

You've made all the decisions to reach where you are today. If you want to live your life differently, choose something that you don't usually choose.

We have the diversity of life. Select the way you want.

Junko

あなたの人生は全て
　　あなたの選択から成っている．

あなたが生きているその人生は
あなたが選んで来た数々の物事で成り立っている．
知らず知らずに決めてきたことや
一生懸命考えて選んだことの結果から
　　　　　　　　今に至っている．
今後生き方を変えたければ
これまで選んで来たこととは違うものを
　　　　　　　敢えて選んでみれば
物事は変わってゆく．
　常に多種多様な選択がある．
　好きな道を進んでいこう．

Admit your weaknesses to be strong

Know what you're good at
and also find what you're not good at.
Understand yourself and work on your weak points
Admitting weaknesses is a part of your strength

自分の弱い部分を認めて強くなろう

自分は何が得意で何が不得意か
自分の苦手な部分や弱い部分を把握し
自分を向上させ改善しよう
自らを良く知り、強化したい部分に努力をしよう
自分の弱さを知ることは立派な強さである、

Let everything come naturally.

Accept everything that shows up in your life
as a gift from the Universe.
Things go smoothly if you let everything come and go naturally.
Quietly notice what or who is coming
and how things are affected by them.
Enjoy the process of taking notes.

全てのものを自然に受け入れよう

目の前に現れたものは、まず拒まず受け入れてみよう。
それからは何らかの縁があって あなたの元にやってきた天からの贈り物
流れには逆らうより沿う方が 物事は自然に進んでゆく。
自分の人生にどんな人や物が現れて
そこから何がどう発展してゆくのか、楽しみながらいこう。

Slowing down doesn't mean giving up.

Doing things at your own speed
or slowing down doesn't mean
 you're quitting.
You can advance at the speed of
 your choice.

ペースを落とすことは諦めることではない。

スピードを落として自分に無理なく何かを進めてゆくことは
物事を諦めることではない。
どんな速度でも前進していることに変わりはない。

Every "No" you get leads to a better place.

If someone refuses you
or someone says "No" to you,
there is no need to be disappointed.
Those are signs for you to have
something better.
If you couldn't pass the job interview,
there is a better position for you
with much better conditions.
If your partner left you,
there is someone that
suits you better.
It's not your fault.
They just weren't
meant to be.
You can look
forward to
better things.

拒絶されることは、
より良い方向に導かれること。

何かを断られたり、誰かに受け入れられなかったり、
一見ショックなことに見えるこれからの事柄は
実はあなたを良い方向へ早く連れて行ってくれる
一種の法則と思おう。

その仕事の面接に落ちたのは
あなたはもっと別の良い場所が
あるということ。

その人と別れたのは
あなたにはもっとふさわしい
素敵な人がいるということ。
だから大丈夫
ご縁がなかっただけ。
次に現れる
素晴らしいものに
わくわくして
いよう。

Too much expectation leads to disappointment.
When you let go of your expectations,
you appreciate every little thing
and wonderful things
start to happen
for you.
If you notice
you're
expecting
too
much,
lower
your
level
of
expec-
tation.
Land of no expectation
has more flowers to offer.

Stop expecting
anything from anyone.

誰にも何にも
期待するのをやめよう

私達は期待しすぎちゃうと上手くゆかなかった時でもがっかりしてしまう。物事はどんどん良い方向に進むけど、それ以上に期待し続けたら、それ以上を期待してしまうから。だから期待している自分に気付いたら、その期待を、もっと下げてみよう。期待のない、どころか、いっぱいくださる、期待のないところ。

Happiness is your choice

Happiness is not a destination in the future.
It is your choice.
If you decide to be happy now,
you'll be happy instantly.

Think about what makes you happy.
If you can live in a bigger house,
would you be happy?
Or as long as you're alive, are you happy?
Take your time and think about it carefully.

幸せはあなたの選択

幸福とはこれからたどり着く場所ではなく
あなたが今すぐここで選べる状態。
私は今幸せだ、と思えば
あなたはもうその瞬間から幸せになれる。
では、一体何から幸せを感じ取れるのだろう
大きくて立派な家に住むのが幸せなのか、
それとも今こうして生きていられるだけで幸せなのか。
自分にとって幸福とは何かを考えてみよう。

Focus on what you had, not on what you lost.

This quote is especially for people who have lost loved ones.
It's sad when you lost someone important.
But please focus on how they existed in your life
and what kind of lessons you've learned from them
instead of focusing on death itself.
Express your gratitude by saying words out loud.

誰かを亡くしたことより、
その人が存在していたという事実に
焦点を合わせよう。

これは特に大切な誰かを失った人達への言葉。
失ったという事実はとても辛いけれど
その人があなたの人生にどのように存在し、どう影響を及ぼし、
自分はそこから何を教わったのかを考え
感謝の気持ちを言葉にしてみよう。

Surrender the urge to control everything in the world.

Even if you'd like to change all the things you don't like in the world, things you can do are very limited.
To reduce your stress, accept the way things are and surrender to your urge to fix and correct everything.

全てのことを自分の思い通りにしたいという気持ちを諦めよう。

気に入らないことを正し、全てを思い通りにしようとしても
私達にできることは限られている。
だから現状をそのまま受け入れ、
何とかしたくなる自分自身に降参しよう
それがストレス減少への道。

Physical attraction fades eventually but soul connection doesn't.

Just like beautiful cherry blossoms bloom for a limited time, our physical attraction has its life.
But the important thing is how we are connected to each other at a soul level.
Real beauty comes from within as we age with our wisdom.
True love is to recognize each other's beauty of mind.

肉体的魅力はやがて消えるが、魂の繋がりは衰えることはない。

綺麗な桜も時期が来れば散るように
私達の外見の魅力にも限りがある。
でも大切なのは見た目ではなく
心でどのように人と繋がっているかということ。
本当の美しさとは内面から滲み出てくるもので
それは学んだ徳が多いほど年相応に輝いてゆく。
お互いの心の美しさを認め合うことが本当の愛。

There is always a sunny side to every difficult situation.

If it looks like something bad has happened to you,
it might have a hidden good meaning
or lead you to a better place.
Even if you don't realize that right away,
think about the true reason for your lesson and its purpose
and how things will go from there.
Look forward to a new place
where this incident leads you.
Hopefully you can proceed with a smile

どんな困難な状況にも必ず良い面がある。

一見大変なことが起きたように見えても
その事実を長い目で見た時
そこには何らかの良い意味合いが含まれている。
そう気づくのがだいぶ後でも、
目の前の問題は一体何のために起こり
どのような方向に流れていくのか、
自分がこの辛い状況を体験しなければならない本当の理由は何か
次に導かれる良い展開を想像して
笑顔で進んでいけるといい。

Sometimes it takes time for everything to make sense

Even if you don't know the meaning of all the things that happen, as time passes, eventually you will be able to understand the whole meaning.

Just like a jigsaw puzzle, all the things happening in your life will make sense as the pieces come together. Be patient while it's taking time.

全ての事柄が意味を成すまで、時間がかかることがある。

意味不明なことが続いたり、納得のいかない状況に陥っても、時間が経てば、その意味や理由がわかるかもしれない。ジグソーパズルの始めでは、完成像が全然想像もつかないように、長い人生に起こる様々な事柄も時間をかけて意味を成すもの。

Pay attention to your own feelings.

When you listen to other people's opinions on your thoughts,
you'll often forget about where they originally started.
Then, when you realize that you're lost yourself.
pause and take a deep breath.
Listen to your own opinions deep inside your heart

自分の感情に注目しよう.

周りに流されると
本当の自分の思いがわからなくなる.
そんな時は立ち止まって深呼吸をしよう.
自分は何を求めているのか
冷静に考えてみよう.

Be proud of how far you've come

No matter how unfortunate you have been,
no matter how hard your life has been,
be proud of how far you've come.
It helped you reach where you are today.
That's your strength and you should be proud.
So you'll be fine from now on, too.
You're much stronger than you think.

ここまで来れた自分に誇りを持とう

これまでにどれほどの不自由をして
どれだけの辛いことがあったとしても、
それらを何とか乗り越えて
今日まで生き抜いて来れた自分に誇りを持とう。
それは明らかにあなたの強さ。
何とかしてここまで来れたのだから
この先も絶対に大丈夫。
自分という人間を改めて見てみると
実は思っていたより凄い人かもしれない。

Great things in life are worth waiting for.

Easy come, easy go.
If something good will happen to you in the future,
it's okay for it to take time.
It's worth the wait.
You'll find something steady and steadfast.

素晴らしいことは待つ甲斐がある。

努力なしに手に入るものは簡単に通り過ぎてゆく。
これからの人生で良いことが起こるならば、
たとえ時間がかかったとしても待つ甲斐があるというもの
時間をかければかけるほど着実にしっかりとしたものが
きちんと手に入る、

You can always reshape and recreate your life.

You can always change anything in your life.
Change your patterns or plans
to make yourself fit to your ideal future
If you're not happy with the way things are right now,
change something and act on it.

自分の人生はいつでも変えられる。

私達はいつでも自分の人生を好きな方に変えていくことができる。
生活習慣を改善したり、計画を立て直して
自分をより理想の姿へ持っていくことができる。
現状に不満があるなら、何らかの行動を起こして
少しずつ自ら何かを変えていこう。

Forgiveness is also for yourself

Forgiveness is not only for the person,
but also for yourself.
Holding grudges makes you feel
heavy and stressful.
it won't make things better.
It's unnecessary to be that way.
But if you forgive and reset your mind,
you'll start to feel better.
Use the precious time of your life
wisely
without dragging your thoughts.

人を許すことは自分のためでもある.

誰かを許すことは
その人のためだけではなく
自分のためでもある。
人を憎んだり妬んだりする感情ほど
無駄なものはない。
それらはあなたを疲れさせる。
でも 人を許して心をリセットすると
綺麗さっぱり気分が軽くなる、
貴重な人生の時間は
他人への重い感情を引きずらず
自分のために 楽しく使おう。

Every goodbye leads to a new hello.

The reason you say goodbye to someone
is to open the opportunity
to meet someone new.
The reason why you leave the situation
is to move on to a more appropriate direction.
Goodbye doesn't mean the end,
but an exciting new start.

全ての別れは新しい出逢いへと繋がる。

別れが来る理由は
次に素敵な人との出逢いが用意されているから。
サヨナラは終わりではなく
より良い出逢いや物事へ繋がる
わくわくするスタート

Life is a journey of finding all about yourself.

It takes a whole life to get to know yourself,
no matter how long you've been living.
If you think you know all about yourself,
you're wrong.

We're all growing and advancing everyday.
So don't judge anything from your experiences.
You never know how you will think of things in the future.
You have abilities and possibilities
that you haven't noticed in yourself yet.
Explorer and go deeper.

人生とは自分探しの旅である。

人は一生をかけて自分を知る。
どれだけ長く生きていても、
自分を知り尽くしていると思ったら間違いである。
あなたはまだ自分の一部しか知らない。
あなたは日々変化し前進しているので
これまでの経験だけで物事を判断しないようにしろ。
あなたにはまだ自分でも気づいていない能力や
果てしない可能性がある。
自分の未知の部分をどんどん探索していこう。

Everyone's different. Respect others.

There is no one in the world
who has the same opinions as you do.
No matter how long you have been together,
no matter how closely you fit,
there is no one who thinks exactly
the way you do.

Don't force your opinions on others
and respect their point of view.
Each of us is a unique individual.

人は皆違う。他人を敬おう。

あなたと全く同じ考えの人間は
この世に誰一人といない。
どんなに長年連れ添った相手でも
どんなに気の合う友達でも
意見が一致するとは限らない。
だからこそ自分の考えや理想を
他人に押し付けず
皆の意見を尊重していこう。
それぞれが個性。

Take it as it comes, no more or no less.

We see things the way we want to see them.
We add up all the stories we perceive as fact
to create our own stress,
but things are no more or no less than
what they actually are.

When you realize that
you're doing the unnecessary,
take a deep breath
and accept the way things simply are.

全てをありのままに受け止めよう
それ以上でも それ以下でもなく。

目の前に見えるものはそこに見えるだけのものであり、
それ以上でもそれ以下でもない。
私達は気付かぬうちに全ての物事に善悪の判断をつけたり、
勝手に味付けをして自分の精神状態を不安定にして
苦しんでいる。

その繰り返しに気づいたら
まずは深呼吸をして、
物事をそのまま受け入れよう。

GEISHA CAT

WOW

Junko

Never forget where you came from.

No matter where you are now,
 never forget where you came from.
Be proud and carry on the pride.
 Don't compare yourself to others.
  Don't try to be someone else
   and find something that you're good at.
  Go on as you are.

自分がどこから来たか、常に忘れずにいよう。

あなたがどこに何年住んでいようとも、
自分がどこから来たかを忘れず、その心と誇りを持って生きてゆこう。
他人と自分を比べず、自分の長所や得意なことを知ろう。
 他の誰かになろうとせず
  自分のそのままの姿を受け入れて進もう。

Balance the give and take of your life.

It's not all about giving and offering yourself to others.
It's okay to receive and have someone help you.
If it's only one way, nothing goes smoothly.
It'll burden you if it's not balanced.
Go slow and see how things are equitable.

人生において、ギブ&テイクのバランスを保とう。

人に何かをしてあげたり、物を与えてあげるだけではなく、
時には人に助けてもらい、何かを受け取ってもいい。
どちらかに偏ると上手くいかない。
日常生活の中でギブ&テイクのバランスが崩れると
どこかで自分に負担がかかってくる。
だから様子を見ながら
　　自分でバランスを調節していこう。

Don't try to change others.
Change yourself around them.

We can't change others
but we can change ourselves.
If we change our attitude around them,
things will go smoother.
Rethink how we are towards others
and make wise decisions.

他人を変えようとするかわりに、
自分の接し方を変えよう。

誰かを変えるのは無理でも
自分の接し方やあり方を変えると
人間関係がスムーズになることがある。
自分のアプローチの仕方、立場、態度を変えて
より上手く人付き合いをしていこう。

Accept and appreciate

It's not easy to accept the way things are.
If you focus on what you have
　　instead of what you're missing,
you'll find something that you feel grateful for.
Find things that you appreciate
　　as many as possible.

現状を受け入れて感謝しよう。

物事をそのまま受け入れることは
　　　　　簡単のようで難しい。
欲しいものや出来ないことではなく、
　既にあるものや今の自分に出来ることに焦点を合わせ、
ありのままの状況の中から
　感謝できる素材をより多く見つけていこう。

Chapter 4: Moving Forward
～前進～

Everyday is a new day.
You can start anything you want.

No matter how you have spent
your life so far,
today is always a new day.
You can start anything you want.
You can change or quit
anything you desire.
It's all up to you.

毎日が新しい日。いつ何を始めてもいい。
昨日まで、どう過ごしていようとも、今日という日は新しい日。
今日から何を始めても、
何を変えても、何を辞めても
それは あなたの自由、

Learn something from every person you meet in your life

There are some people you like or dislike for whatever reason...
people you see often or people you don't see much.
a delivery guy from post office,
your neighbor lady, school teacher or boss.
When you know that you can learn something from anyone,
every encounter becomes more compelling.

人生で出逢う全ての人達から何かを学ぼう.

好きな人, 嫌いな人, どうでもいい人,
いつも会う人, たまにしか会わない人,
郵便屋さん, 近所のおばさん, 学校の先生, 職場の上司,
どんな人からも何でも学べると思えば
誰との出逢いも全て興味深いものとなる.

Talk about your dreams and visions

Find friends whom you can talk to about your dreams and future plans. You'll enjoy life more.

Be with people who encourage you instead of stopping you. Your goal will be reached sooner.

あなたの夢やビジョンを語ろう、

将来の夢や未来の計画を語り合える仲間を見つけられると
人生は楽しくなる。
あなたの考えを馬鹿にせず、否定せず、
応援してくれる友達が周りにいると
より一層理想へ近付くことができる。

If there's no road, create your own.

When you want to start something new,
but can't find anyone who did it before,
be a brave pioneer.
It's not impossible just because no one did it before.
You have a great chance to be successful
because no one has ever done it.
Someone might follow your path in the near future.

道がなければ自分で作ろう。

何かを始める時、
前例がなければ その第一人者になろう。
進みたい方向への道が見えなくても
自分で何とか開拓していこう。
前例がないから不可能なのではなく、
前例がないからこそ 大成功する可能性がある。
あなたの作る道を
この先誰かが たどるかもしれない。

Once you stop worrying, everything will be okay.

Don't ruin your chances by worrying too much.
Don't spend your present time having fears.
Worrying makes no progress.
If you think you'll be okay,
things will be fine.

心配するのをやめれば全て上手くいく、

まだ何も始まっていないのに心配ばかりして
せっかくのチャンスを台無しにしないようにしよう。
先のことを不安に思い過ぎて
今楽しむのを忘れないようにしよう。
何がどうなるかわからないと心配ばかりしていては
良い結果へ自分を導くことは出来ない。
大丈夫と思って進めば上手くいくもの。

Do it now.
Someday might never come.

If you have something in your mind,
something that you always wanted to try,
do it today.
Even if you can't do it all at once,
Start with one step today.
Because another day might never come.
Your time is now.

今やろう いつかという日は
　　　　　来ないかもしれない

いつかやろうと思ってずっと心の中にあることを、今日やってみよう。
一度にできないことでも、今日から少しずつやってみよう。
いつかやりたいと思い続けていても、その日は来ないかもしれない。
だからこそ今、行動を起こそう。

Reinvent yourself everyday.

Try something today
to be smarter than you were yesterday.
If you make an effort everyday,
your possibilities will be expanded.

毎日自分を改革しよう.

昨日より より賢い自分になるため
今日何らかの努力をしよう.
毎日自分を磨いていれば
あらゆる可能性が どんどん広がってゆく.

Be different, be you

You can't express your true self
by copying or meeting anyone's expectations.
Be different from others
and make yourself valuable.
Do something that only you can do
and be confident.

人と違った自分らしさを持とう

誰かの真似をしたり
人に言われるままの行動をしていると
そこにはせっかくのあなたの個性も
人格も表現できない。
この世に生まれてきた以上、
他人とは違うことをして
あなたの存在に価値を生み出そう。

No need to get anyone's approval to do what you want.

You can do anything you want without anyone's approval.
Don't lose your true self by listening to too many people around you.

自分のやりたいことをやるには、誰からの承認も不要。

いちいち誰かに相談して同意や許可を求めなくても
あなたのやりたいことは実行できる。
周りの意見に惑わされて
本当の自分を見失わないようにしよう。

Trust your unknown future

Your unknown future has infinite possibilities.
Be excited for what's coming instead of having fears
Your excitement leads you to amazing future adventures.

未知の未来を信じよう.
まだ何がどう成るかわからない行く先には
無限の可能性が秘められている
その着地に不安を持つのではなく
わくわくドキドキしながら進んでいけば
素敵な未来に繋がってゆく

Achieve small goals to build your confidence.

You don't need to do anything vast.
Achieving small daily goals will make you confident.
And confidence will lead to big successes.

小さな目標を達成し続けて自信を付けよう。

何か大きなことをしなくてもいい。
日々の小さな成功の積み重ねが
自信に繋がってゆく。
そしてその自信はあなたを大きな成功へと導く。

Follow the flow of life.

Things will pass by that aren't meant to be
but things will stay when they are meant to be.
Life has its natural stream.
You won't reach anywhere
　　　　if you go against it.
　　　Go with the flow.

人生の流れに沿っていこう。

自分に縁のないものは次第に離れてゆくが
縁のあるものは遅かれ早かれあなたの元へやってくる。
人生には自然の流れがあり
それに背いてもどこにも進めない。
流れに沿っていこう。

Freedom is everything

You can't be true to yourself
if there's no freedom.
You can't use your creativity
if you can't be yourself.
Unblock yourself from certain rules
and allow yourself to be creative and free.

自由こそが全て

自由のないところに
あなたの本来の姿は存在しない。
自分の望むことが不可能な場所では
あなたの本領を発揮できず
素晴らしいものは生まれて来ない。
様々な枠や決まりごとから自分を解放して
自らの手で自由を創り出そう

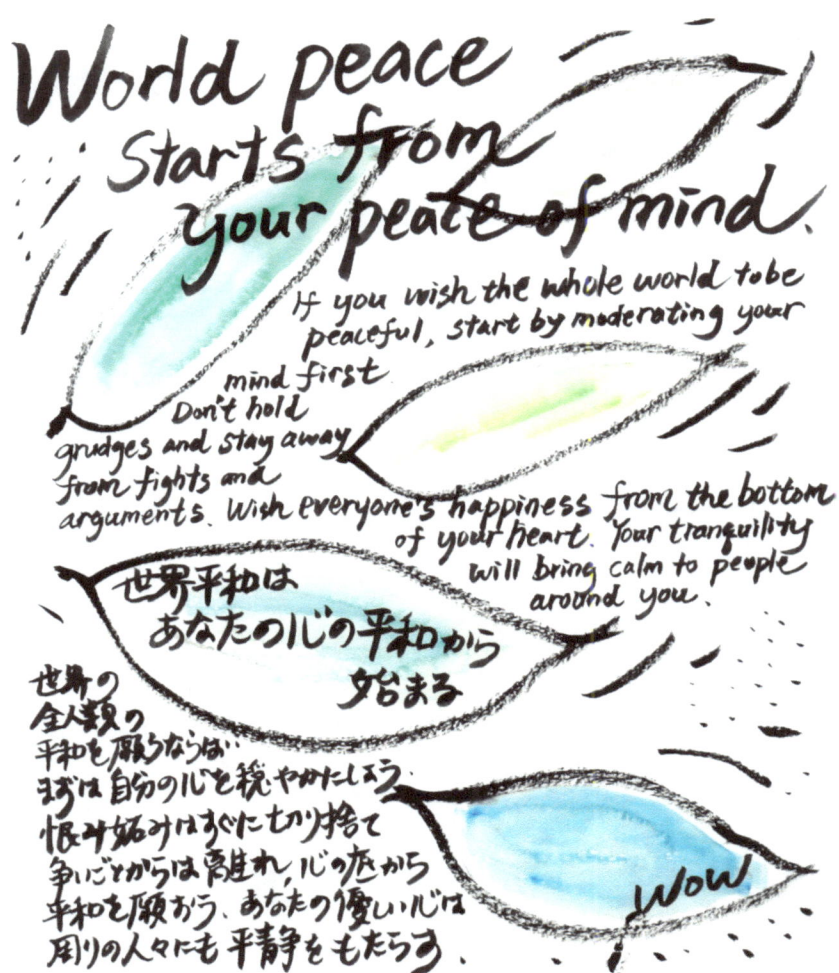

World peace starts from your peace of mind.

If you wish the whole world to be peaceful, start by moderating your mind first. Don't hold grudges and stay away from fights and arguments. Wish everyone's happiness from the bottom of your heart. Your tranquility will bring calm to people around you.

世界平和は
あなたの心の平和から
始まる

世界の全人類の平和を願うなら、まずは自分の心を穏やかにしよう。恨み妬みはすぐに切り捨て争いごとからは離れ、心の底から平和を願おう。あなたの優しい心は周りの人々にも平静をもたらす

wow

Be the person that you want to be.

How would you like to live your life?
Will you always obey others?
Will you always be trying to meet someone's expectations?
Who are you acting for?
Did you foresee the present that you're currently living?
Check your heart for your ideal future.

なりたい自分になろう.

自分はどんなふうに生きていきたいのか.
他人の言いなりに進んでいくのか.
誰かの期待に応えながらいくのか.
自分の行動は誰のためか.
今の自分は過去に思い描いていた自分だろうか.
常に自分の理想を確認していこう.

It's always okay to change your mind.

No one can control what you think.
You can change your opinions anytime
no matter how long you had them
in your mind.
You're the only person
who's in charge of your thoughts.

いつ心変わりしても大丈夫。

あなたの心は他の誰にも管理されていない。
たとえ自分で長い間心に決めてきたことでも
いつ意見を変えてもいい。
あなたの思考をコントロールしているのは
自分一人だけ。

Little things matter.
They might become big things later.

If you ignore small things now,
you might regret them later.
They might not seem important to you now,
but they may have a big effect
on your life in the future.

些細なことでも、
後に大きな意味を持つかもしれない

今目の前にある小さなことを無視したら
後になって後悔するかもしれない。
それがこの時点で大切なことに思えなくても
将来あらゆることに影響を及ぼし
重要な意味を成す可能性もある

Face forward and move on.

You're standing here facing forward.
Looking back won't change anything.
Have hopes for the future
and keep going forward.

前を向いて進んでいこう

今ここにいるあなたは前を向いて立っている。
過去を振り返って後悔しても何も変わらない。
だから過去にはこだわらず、未来に希望を持ち、
しっかり前を向いて進んでいこう。

If you fall down, just get up.

Even if you fall down,
You always have a choice to get up.
It's up to you to either keep spending your life crying,
or to get up quickly and move on.
You admit weaknesses when you fall
but be proud of your strengths
when you get up.

転んでも起き上がればいい。

転んで倒れたとしても立ち上がればいい。
地面で倒れたまま泣き叫び続けて
人生の貴重な時間を費すのも.
起き上がってまたすぐに歩き出すのも
全て自分次第。
転べば弱い自分に気付くことができ、
立ち上がれば強い自分に誇りを持つことができる。

All the answers are within you.

Friends give you lots of advice when you don't know what to do, but you're the one who decides what to do in the end.
Deep inside, you already know the answer.
Don't lose it by getting confused by common sense or other people's opinions.
Be calm and ask yourself.

全ての答えはあなたの中にある.

何をどうして良いかわからず
誰かに相談して何を言われたとしても
最終的にどうするか決めるのは自分.
本当は何をどうしたいのか
あなたは心の奥でわかっているはず
他人の意見や世間の常識に惑わされて
自分の答えを失くしてしまわないように
静かに自分の胸に問いかけることを忘れずに.

Have hopes.

Always carry hopes with you
no matter where you go.
The future is bright
as long as you don't give up.
Don't forget to have hopes
by believing in what lies ahead.

希望を持とう。

常に希望を持っていこう。
諦めた途端、全ての可能性は消え去るが
諦めない限り将来は明るい。
自分の未来を信じて
希望を忘れずにいこう。

Proceed with assurance

Don't doubt your own decisions
and proceed with assurance
People will be influenced by your determined attitude
and will support you.
All roads will be open
and things become possible
when you're confident.
Start doing one by one
and become courageous

確信を持って進んでいこう

自分の決断を疑わず
確信を持って進んでいこう
あなたの凛とした言動に
人々は影響され
応援してくれる
自信溢れるところには道が開け
あらゆることが可能となる
ひとつずつできることからこなして
自信に繋げていこう
信じるところに成功は訪れる

Do whatever you want. It's your life!

No matter what people say,
do whatever you want
as long as you're responsible.
Do what makes you feel good
and go see whomever you desire.
Seek the most enjoyment
from your precious life.

自分の人生、好きなようにやろう。

誰に何と言われようとも
他人に迷惑をかけない限り
あなたの人生は好きなように生きればいい。
やりたいことをやり、
会いたい人に会い、
後悔のない満ち足りた人生を送ろう。
貴重な人生を満喫して
思いっきり楽しもう。

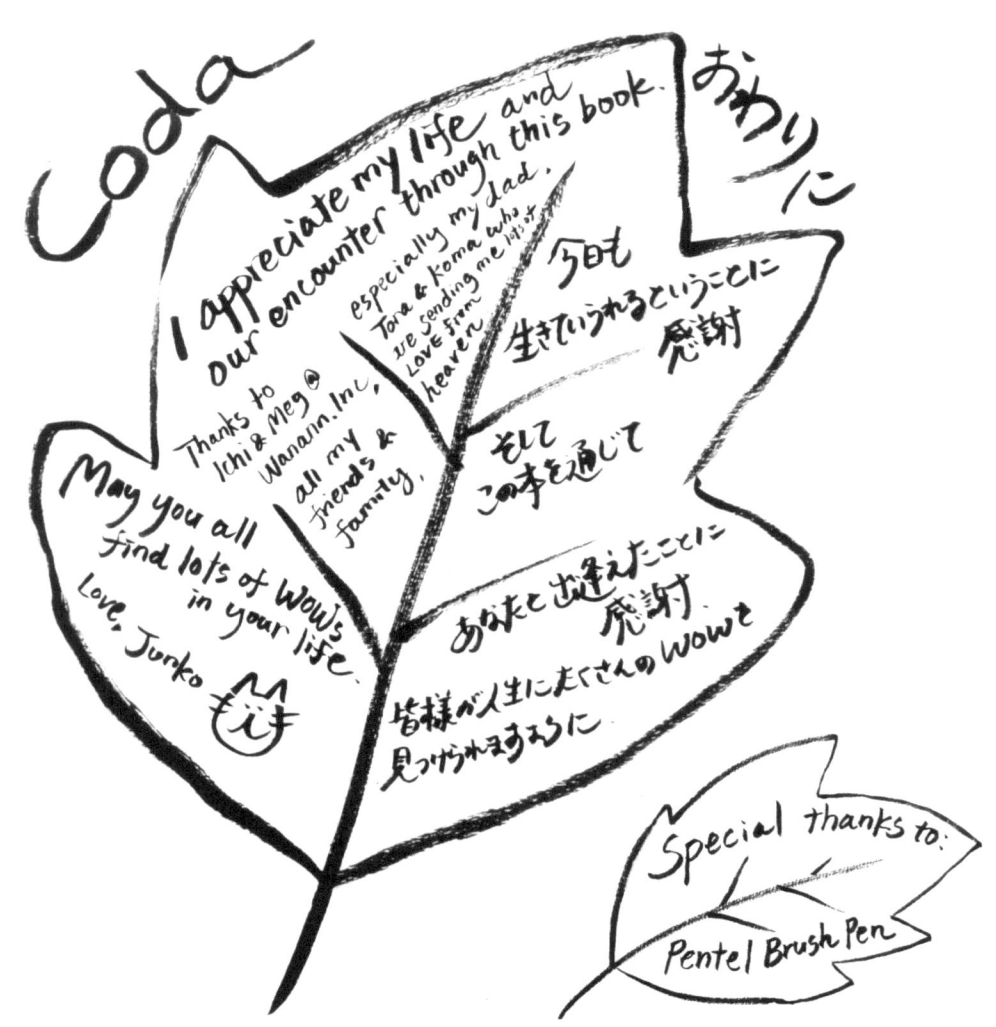

About The Author

Junko (pronounced June-Ko) is the creative director of her own brand, Wow By Junko. She is from Hokkaido in northern Japan. Her parents named her Junko because she was born in June. Her name's Chinese characters 純子 mean "pure child." She's living freely just like her name.

Junko's online store carries her whimsical and unique designs. Please check the link below.

https://wowbyjunko.bigcartel.com
Instagram: wow_by_junko

Junko's Furry Friends

Pudding: Bird Angel

Tora: Cat Angel

Koma aka Meowsy:
Cat Angel

Irish: Zen Cat Model

著者について

Junkoは、独自のブランド、Wow By Junkoのクリエイティブ・ディレクターで北海道出身です。6月（June）に生まれたので両親にJunkoと名付けられました。漢字表記は純子で、その名前の通り純粋な子供のように自由に暮らしています。

Junkoのオンラインストアでは、彼女の独特でユニークなデザインの商品が扱われています。インスタグラムと共に上記よりご確認ください。

- My favorite word
- My name
- My favorite place
- My favorite color
- My favorite food
- My favorite thing to do
- My favorite animal
- My favorite song
- My favorite flower
- My dreams and visions
- My favorite person

WOW
by Junko

AMESIAN BOOKS
2535 W. 237th St., Unit 106
Torrance, CA 90505
amesianbooks.com

Copyright © 2020 by Junko, AMESIAN BOOKS
All rights reserved.

AMESIAN BOOKS is a division of Wanann, Inc.
No part of this publication may be reproduced, stored, or transmitted in any form or by any means, electronic, mechanical, photocopied, recorded or otherwise, without prior written consent from the publisher.
Notice of Disclaimer: The information contained in this book is based on the author's experience and options. The author and publisher will not be held liable for the use or misuse of the information in this book.

Publisher: Kyoichi Ichimura

Art director: Kyoichi Ichimura
DTP: Megumi Tamura
Studio assistant: Anna Nakamura

Sales and distribution: Risa Akashi

Words, photos and illustrations by Junko

ISBN 978-1-945352-04-1 (PB)   ISBN 978-1-945352-05-8 (EB)

2 4 6 8 10 9 7 5 3 1

First edition, 2020

Amesian Books
WANANN, Inc.

www.ingramcontent.com/pod-product-compliance
Lightning Source LLC
Chambersburg PA
CBHW050753110526
44592CB00003B/52